POTBELLIED PIG

Potbellied Pig Care, Training, Temperament, Feeding, Costs, Senses And Health Care

Gregory Scott

Table of Contents

CHAPTER ONE 3
- POTBELLIED PIG 3
- CAN YOU OWN A POT BELLIED PIG? 4

CHAPTER TWO 7
- POTBELLIED PIG BEHAVIOR AND TEMPERAMENT 7
- HOUSING 11
- NEEDS FOR PARTICULAR SUBSTRATE 13
- WHAT DO POTBELLIED PIGS EAT & DRINK? .14

CHAPTER THREE 17
- COMMON HEALTH PROBLEMS 17
- EXERCISE 20
- GROOMING 21
- INFORMATION ON SIZE 23

CHAPTER FOUR 26
- PROS & CONS OF KEEPING A POTBELLIED PIG AS A PET 26
- PURCHASING YOUR POTBELLIED PIG 27

THE END 29

CHAPTER ONE

POTBELLIED PIG

People usually think of potbellied pigs as farm animals, but they can be sweet, smart, and loving pets.

A potbellied pig can definitely be a well-loved pet if it gets the right care and training.

But some people can't keep a pig as a pet because they don't know how much work it is.

Since pigs are smart and like to explore, it can be hard to keep them busy.

Also, because pigs are always hungry, it can be hard to make sure they eat well.

Overall, you can expect to spend a lot of time with your pet pig each day.

You will also need to play with it and take it outside to keep it moving.

CAN YOU OWN A POT BELLIED PIG?
Legality

Potbellied pigs are allowed in many places, but in some, they are considered livestock and need special housing and permits.

In some places, pigs can be kept as pets as long as they are on a leash or in a closed-off outdoor area.

Since pigs are legal livestock in most states, you'll need to pay close attention to the laws in your area.

Ethics

Most of the time, whether or not it's right to own an animal depends on whether or not you can give it what it needs to be healthy.

Potbellied pigs need a lot of room, care, friends, and things to do to keep their minds active.

As long as you can give your pig everything it needs, it would be moral for you to have one.

Things To Consider

There are different sizes of potbellied pigs, which can be a problem if you think you're getting a cute little piglet but end up with a 200-pound pet instead.

Do your research, know what you're getting, and think about whether you can handle or even want a pet this big.

CHAPTER TWO

POTBELLIED PIG BEHAVIOR AND TEMPERAMENT

Some people think that having a dog and a pig are the same thing.

Even though pigs and dogs are both social and playful, they also have their own habits.

Pigs learn quickly and are smart.

They can be taught to go to the bathroom, walk on a leash, and even do some tricks.

But they are often stubborn and sensitive.

To get them to work with you, you need to give them a lot of positive reinforcement, especially treats.

A pig is very smart, so if it doesn't have enough to do and people to talk to, it will get bored and might do something bad.

Pigs are naturally curious and like to use their noses to look for food.

This can make them mess up your yard and knock over things in your house.

You can stop this by hiding some of their daily food in treat puzzles or in a part of your yard where you don't mind them digging.

Like dogs, pigs can form close bonds with people.

They can also learn to get along with other animals in the house, especially if they are raised with them from a young age.

In fact, it's usually better to have more than one pig because they like to hang out together.

Pet pigs like it when their owners scratch and rub them, and many of them will sit next to you and cuddle.

They are usually friendly, but if they feel threatened, scared, or protective of their territory, they can be mean to people or other animals.

Getting your pig spayed or neutered can help you control hormones that can make it aggressive.

Also, pigs can make some very loud noises to show how they feel.

A pig is not a good pet if you want something quiet.

To learn to respect their owners, pigs need rules and limits.

This is one of the best things you can do for your pet pig.

Always praise good behavior and try to change or say "no" to bad behavior.

To raise a potbellied pig that gets along well with its family and is well-behaved, you have to do things over and over again and be patient.

HOUSING

Pigs are smart and curious, so you'll need to "pig-proof" any areas of your house where the pig will go, just like you would for a toddler.

Cover the electrical outlets, make sure the stairs are out of bounds, and get rid of things like cords and rugs that could cause someone to trip.

Pigs are pretty clean animals, but they can be destructive if they don't have enough of their own toys to play with.

You can even teach your pig to go to the bathroom in a litter box or outside by giving it compliments or healthy treats.

Give your pig a place of its own, like a big tent or crate.

When a pig has its own space, it can feel calmer.

Also, it's best to give your pig an indoor rooting box with rocks and other natural materials where it can use its snout to look for small pieces of food you put in the box.

Lastly, your pig needs to move around a lot so it doesn't get constipated. It should be able to play and walk outside often.

NEEDS FOR PARTICULAR SUBSTRATE

If you go to a farm, you'll see pigs in a pen covered in hay.

If you keep your pig outside, hay can be a good place for it to sleep.

It's not necessary, especially if you let your pig sleep inside.

You can also use pine shavings, wood chips, leaves, and other things if you don't have any nearby.

WHAT DO POTBELLIED PIGS EAT & DRINK?

When it comes to getting food, pigs can be just as stubborn as they are known to be.

They can learn how to open the fridge, cabinets, and pantry, or anywhere else they think food might be hiding.

They can also be demanding, like when they beg for food or attack people who have food.

Pig pellets, which are high in fiber and low in protein and fat, are what your pig should eat.

Follow the directions on the bag of pellets and ask your vet how much to give.

Also, 25% of the pig's daily food should be fresh vegetables that are not starchy.

For fiber, you can give your pet pig alfalfa hay or bran, and many veterinarians recommend giving it a multivitamin.

Many pig owners feed their pigs in a bowl twice a day, in the morning and in the evening.

Some of the pig's daily food was also put in a rooting area to keep the pig's mind busy.

In fact, by rooting around in the dirt, your pig can get minerals like iron and selenium.

Lastly, always have a big bowl of fresh water out.

CHAPTER THREE

COMMON HEALTH PROBLEMS

Because pigs eat a lot, it's easy to give them too much food.

Many adult pigs are too fat, which can cause arthritis and other serious illnesses.

If the fat rolls over your pig's eyes, it means the animal is too heavy.

If that's the case, talk to your vet about your pig's diet and don't feed it any table scraps or foods that are too salty or fatty.

Make sure that everyone in your home agrees that the pig shouldn't get extra treats.

Usually, something is wrong if your pig stops eating.

An infection or a blockage in the digestive system could be to blame.

If this happens, you should go to the vet as soon as possible.

When pigs are too hot, they might be sad, not move around much, and lay down.

They may also breathe with their mouths open or pant, and they may start out with a fever that goes down to a temperature lower than normal.

If you see this happening, give the pig a place to go where it will be cool and out of the sun.

Also, pigs with light skin are more likely to get burned by the sun and get skin cancer.

When they go outside, it's best to give them some shade and put sunscreen on them.

One of the most common diseases in potbellied pigs is mange, which is caused by mites.

Pigs with mange have dry, scaly, and itchy skin.

If you see this, your pig needs to go to the vet.

The animal should be checked on once a year by a vet who specializes in potbellied pigs.

The hooves of a pig also need to be trimmed often to keep its feet and legs from getting hurt.

EXERCISE

A potbellied pig needs to have both its mind and body worked on.

Pigs get most of their exercise from roaming around and digging for food, so it's important to give your pig a lot of space to do these things.

Your pig should be doing something active at least once a day, like looking for food, putting together puzzles, or exploring their outdoor pen.

Your pig can also learn to walk on a leash with you.

This is another great way for their hooves to naturally wear down.

GROOMING

Even though pigs have a bad rep for being dirty, they are pretty clean on their own.

Still, they will need to be brushed often to keep their bristly hair under control and get rid of flaky skin.

Give them a bath about once a week in your tub or outside using baby shampoo or shampoo made just for pigs.

You should start cleaning their ears and the skin around their eyes when they are young so that it is easy for both of you to feel safe and calm while grooming.

INFORMATION ON SIZE

It's important to know how big a pet pig will get before you get one.

Most of the time, potbellied pigs are put into groups based on their size, but the groups have different names, weights, and heights.

These are the most common sizes:

• Potbellied pigs, Vietnamese potbellied pigs, Kunekune pigs, and Chinese potbellied pigs usually grow to be 16 to 26 inches tall and weigh between 125 and 200 pounds.

Miniature potbellied pigs can weigh up to 100 pounds and are 15 to 16 inches tall.

Most teacup potbellied pigs are 14.5 inches tall and weigh between 35 and 45 pounds.

Toy potbellied pigs can be 14 inches tall and weigh up to 35 to 40 pounds.

• Royal Dandies are about 15 inches tall and weigh between 29 and 39 pounds as adults.

- Micro Mini Pigs can be anywhere from 18 to 30 pounds heavy and 10 to 12.5 inches tall.

- Dandie Extremes stand 12 inches tall and weigh between 12 and 29 pounds.

- Mini Julianas are between 8 and 12.5 inches tall and 15 to 28 pounds.

Breeders who are not honest may breed pigs before they are fully grown and say that the babies will grow up to be the same size as the parents.

CHAPTER FOUR

PROS & CONS OF KEEPING A POTBELLIED PIG AS A PET

Potbellied pigs are smart and loving animals that can make great pets if you can give them what they need and a good place to live.

Long-term, a potbellied pig's playful nature can make your life better, but you should think about whether you have the time, energy, money, and space to take care of one.

PURCHASING YOUR POTBELLIED PIG

Always get a pig from a reputable breeder or rescue group.

Rescue groups take in a lot of pigs whose owners didn't know how to care for them.

Rescues can help you find a pig that suits your lifestyle.

Don't buy a pig over the internet or any other way that doesn't let you meet the animal first.

Also, try to talk to people who have gotten an animal from the breeder or rescue to find out how their experiences were.

The person selling you the pig should know a lot about its background, health, and personality.

Find a pig that is friendly, awake, and bright.

Red flags include a pig that doesn't want to eat or one that doesn't move.

From a breeder, you can expect to pay an average of $500 and less from a rescue group.

THE END

Ingram Content Group UK Ltd.
Milton Keynes UK
UKHW022059230323
419066UK00015B/878